MAIN DISHES — BEEF

MAIN DISHES - LAMB

MAIN DISHES - FISH

MAIN DISHES - PORK

MAIN DISHES - CHICKEN & TURKEY

CHEESE & EGGS

VEGETABLES

SALADS & SALAD DRESSINGS

POTATOES, BAKED BEANS...34

HOT BREADS...34,35

DESSERTS

BREAKFASTS

PARTIES & HOLIDAYS

DIPS & HORS D'OEUVRES...49

Beef 'N' Sour Cream

for two

Melt:

1 Tablespoon Margarine

IN A MED. SIZE SKILLET OVER LOW HEAT

add:

½ Med.-Sized Onion, Chopped

TURN HEAT TO MED. AND COOK TILL ONION IS LIMP (2-3 min.)

Then add:

¼ Cup Dry White Wine

TURN HEAT DOWN AND SIMMER FOR 5 MINUTES

Then stir in:

1 Can (12 oz.) Libby's Roast Beef with Gravy

SIMMER ANOTHER 5 MINUTES

Add and stir in:

¼ Cup Sour Cream (save leftover sour cream for tomorrow's baked potatoes)

HEAT BUT DO NOT BOIL.

Serve on toast cut in half ◩ or on rice.

Good with Birdseye frozen green beans with almonds and grapefruit cup salad (P. 30)

②

DINNER FOR TWO* in one Pan

Put about a Tablespoon of Mazola or Wesson Oil **in a skillet** start with burner on <u>high</u>, then turn to <u>medium</u> after it's hot. Now **DUMP IN:**

1 lb. ground beef (preferably chuck or round)

CHOP THE MEAT UP AS IT BROWNS, USING A BIG SPOON.

POUR OFF GREASE AND DISCARD. THE WAY TO DO THIS IS TO PUT A LID ON THE PAN AND TILT THE PAN SIDEWAYS OVER AN EMPTY CAN. SLIDE THE LID OFF THE PAN JUST ENOUGH TO HOLD THE MEAT IN WHILE LETTING THE GREASE OUT. PUT THE CAN OF GREASE INTO THE REFRIG. TO HARDEN — THEN THROW AWAY.

ADD TO BROWNED MEAT:
1 pkg. (12 oz.) **frozen mixed vegetables** DON'T THAW
½ tiny can of V-8

Put lid on pan. Leave cooking for about ½ hour, turning burner to **low** after vegetables have thawed and separated. At this time, <u>stir</u>.

STIR AGAIN - WELL - WHEN COOKED.

SPREAD OVER TOP: ½ can (undiluted) **Campbell's Cheddar Cheese Soup**

Put lid back on. Turn stove to simmer till ready to eat (or turn off.) Stir before serving.

Good served with tiny can (containing six) Pillsbury biscuits
AND AMBROSIA DESSERT

* Can be stretched to serve 4 by adding 1 can (about 1 lb.) Franco-American spaghetti last 5-10 minutes of cooking.

③

READ FIRST

The conventional way of broiling steaks is: Turn the broiler (upper heating element in the oven) to "BROIL" (high) and cook the steaks near the top of the oven quickly, under intense heat, turning the meat over once, leaving the oven door cracked open. This causes a lot of spattering and dries out the meat.

SEE BETTER WAY ON OPPOSITE PAGE.

HINTS FOR COOKING JUICIER, TASTIER STEAKS, no matter which method you choose:

DO NOT SALT STEAKS UNTIL READY TO EAT. Salt draws out juices during cooking.

TRIM OFF MOST OF FAT. (Leave only a tiny edge of fat on meat, to prevent drying out during cooking.)

RUB SOFT MARGARINE (or oil) OVER MEAT TO KEEP IT FROM DRYING OUT WHILE COOKING.

DO NOT PREHEAT BROILER.

LEAVE OVEN DOOR CRACKED OPEN WHILE BROILING.

GET STEAKS THE SAME THICKNESS. The ideal thickness for this type of cooking is one inch.

If you can cook a steak, bake a potato, and toss a salad, you've got it made.

See:
SALADS.......... page 29
POTATOES........ page 34

④

PeRFecT STeaK *every time*

LAMB CHOPS CAN BE COOKED THIS WAY, TOO!

Read opposite page first.

You won't believe this! But once you have tried cooking steaks this way, you will never want to change (except to cook them outdoors sometime – and that's your husband's department.)

SELECT STEAKS ONE INCH THICK (important)
(club, T-bone, rib, sirloin, porterhouse, or filet)

PLACE ON COLD BROILER RACK IN PAN LINED WITH FOIL

Rub Chiffon margarine on both sides of meat.

Gas Stove: Put meat on top shelf
Electric: Put meat 5-6 inches from top heating coils

Don't preheat broiler.

SET BROILER ON 300° (Surprised?)
Leave oven door cracked open.

COOK ON EACH SIDE 12 MIN., turning only once.

THEN CHANGE SETTING TO "BROIL" for just a minute or so, till your steak is brown on top.
DON'T TURN!
You now have RARE STEAK.

Like it better done?
Leave it in longer.

⑤

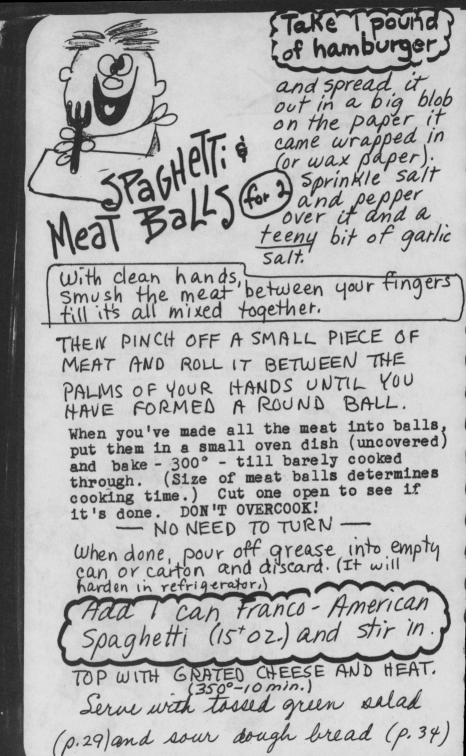

Take 1 pound of hamburger

SPAGHETTi & Meat Balls (for 2)

and spread it out in a big blob on the paper it came wrapped in (or wax paper). Sprinkle salt and pepper over it and a _teeny_ bit of garlic salt.

With clean hands, smush the meat between your fingers till it's all mixed together.

THEN PINCH OFF A SMALL PIECE OF MEAT AND ROLL IT BETWEEN THE PALMS OF YOUR HANDS UNTIL YOU HAVE FORMED A ROUND BALL.

When you've made all the meat into balls, put them in a small oven dish (uncovered) and bake - 300° - till barely cooked through. (Size of meat balls determines cooking time.) Cut one open to see if it's done. DON'T OVERCOOK!
—— NO NEED TO TURN ——

When done, pour off grease into empty can or carton and discard. (It will harden in refrigerator.)

Add 1 can Franco-American Spaghetti (15+ oz.) and stir in.

TOP WITH GRATED CHEESE AND HEAT. (350°-10 min.)
Serve with tossed green salad (p. 29) and sour dough bread (p. 34)

6

CHILI Pie

Bakes in 10 minutes

Here's what you need:

- 2½ cups of <u>Fritos</u> Corn Chips (ANY SIZE - DON'T CRUNCH UP)
- 1 large <u>onion,</u> chopped up fine
- 1 (15 oz.) can of <u>Chili</u> (NO BEANS!)
- 1 cup grated Amer. cheese (sharp)
  YOU CAN BUY IT ALREADY GRATED IN PLASTIC BAGS

Put 1½ cups Fritos in baking dish. Sprinkle onions and half the grated cheese on top of Fritos.

POUR HEATED CHILI OVER THAT.

Put rest of Fritos + cheese on top. **BAKE AT 350°** (uncovered) 10 min.

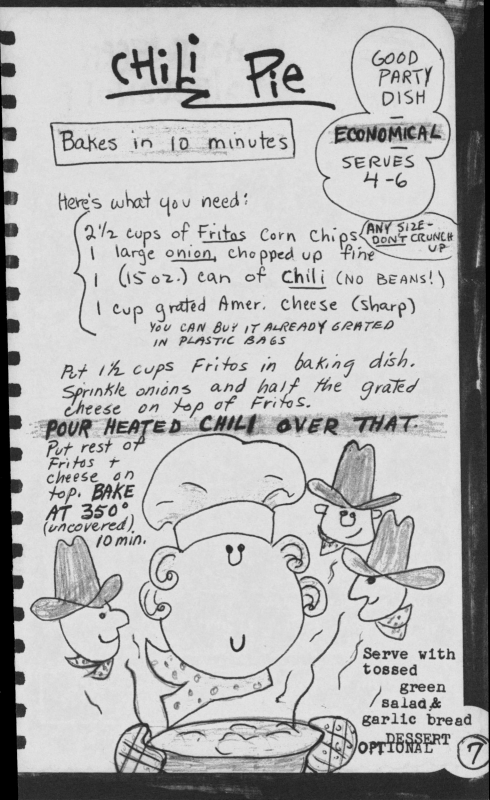

Serve with tossed green salad & garlic bread

DESSERT OPTIONAL

7

HAMBURGER STROGANOFF

Serves 4-6, or you can feed 2 and freeze the leftovers.

Put about a Tablespoon of vegetable oil (Mazola, Wesson, etc.) in a skillet. MED. HEAT.

ADD TO SKILLET:

1 POUND OF GROUND BEEF Chuck or round, if you can afford it.

BREAK IT UP WITH A SPOON AS YOU STIR IT AROUND WHILE IT COOKS. WHEN IT IS BARELY BROWN, POUR OFF GREASE (into old can — and discard after it has hardened in refrig.)

Remove skillet from heat.

STIR IN:

1 ENVELOPE (1½oz.) STROGANOFF MIX

1 CAN (8oz.) TOMATO SAUCE WITH MUSHROOMS

1 CUP MILK

PUT BACK ON <u>MED.</u> HEAT TILL HEATED THROUGH, THEN REDUCE HEAT AND SIMMER 10 MINUTES.

Serve over Minute Rice or noodles or toast.

Serve with frozen chopped spinach and sliced tomatoes

8

LeG of LaMB & BeeF RoaST

"NEVER SEAR, SALT, OR BASTE A ROAST!" ...Adelle Davis in
Let's Cook it Right

You'll need:

(1) A roasting rack (Teflon, if possible)

(2) A shallow pan to hold rack and
      catch drippings. (Line with foil.)

(3) Salad oil to rub over the roast.

(4) A meat thermometer. (Get at supermarket or dept. store.)

Leave meat out for half an hour so it will be
room temperature. Then rub oil over it. Insert meat
thermometer deep into meat, avoiding fat or bone.

Leg of Lamb:	25-30 min. per lb. (well done)
Beef Roast:	18-20 min. per lb. (med. rare)

OVEN 350°

Exception: rolled roasts need 5-10 min. longer per pound.

Ovens vary, so cooking time varies. This is just a guide.
Trust your meat thermometer! It has markings for the
desired internal temperature of any kind of meat you're
cooking, showing rare, medium, and well done for beef.

SAVE ANY JUICES COLLECTED IN PAN FOR GRAVY   skim off
melted fat first) AND FOR LEFTOVER RECIPES (below). Any
juices you don't use right away, cover and refrigerate.
As drippings cool, any fat you missed will rise to top.
Scrape it off and discard before using juices again.
(You can freeze leftover juices.)

GRAVY:

Into a skillet put:

2 Tablespoons salad oil (Get it hot.)
2 Tablespoons flour (Turn to Med.-Low.)
Cook, stirring, for 3-5 minutes. Then add juices a little
at a time, stirring and watching to see how much gravy
thickens. Give it time! Add more drippings until gravy
is consistency you like. If you have insufficient juices,
use water or beer to piece out with. (Stale beer is okay.)
Salt to taste.

LefTOVeR LaMB oR BeeF:

Make gravy as above. Then cut up coarsely and add:

2 stems of washed celery (about 3/4 cup)
Same amount of green pepper (also washed first)

Now add:

About 2 cups of bite-size leftover lamb or beef
      (Remove any fat or gristle.)

Optional: 1/3 teaspoon or more curry powder
Salt only if needed.

Serve over
rice or
noodles

Simmer 20-30 minutes, covered, stirring occasionally.

BuSY DaY ReCIPe!

IN A BIG HURRY? Just heat leftover meat hunks in Compliment
Swiss Steak Sauce and serve over Minute Rice. Delicious!

9

PiNeaPPLe PoRK CHOPS

(FOR TWO)

TRIM FAT FROM:

4 pork chops

SPRINKLE THEM HEAVILY WITH:
salt & pepper

Always cook pork till the pink is gone — but don't overcook till dry! NEVER SERVE PINK PORK (It's dangerous)

COVER THE BOTTOM OF A FRYING PAN WITH:
French dressing. (GOOD SEASONS IS GOOD!)

TURN BURNER ON **HIGH**.

Quickly:
SEAR (BROWN) **CHOPS** ON EACH SIDE.

(UNTIL THEY ARE DARK BROWN IN SPOTS)

REDUCE HEAT TO SIMMER.

Open:
Tiny can of **crushed pineapple** (Pour off juice)
DUMP IT ON TOP OF CHOPS. (Use it all if you want to.)

Put lid on, and **SIMMER UNTIL TENDER** when punched
with fork. (Depends on thickness of chops.)
(Try 20 minutes.)

GOOD WiTH STeaMeD CaBBaGe
(p. 27)

AND BaKeD PoTaToeS (p. 34)

(10)

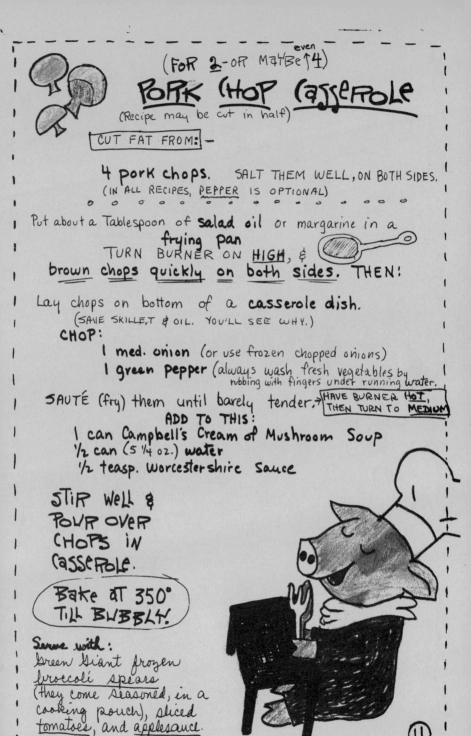

(FOR 2 OR MAYBE even 4)

PORK CHOP CASSEROLE

(Recipe may be cut in half)

CUT FAT FROM: —

4 pork chops. SALT THEM WELL, ON BOTH SIDES.
(IN ALL RECIPES, PEPPER IS OPTIONAL)

Put about a Tablespoon of **salad oil** or margarine in a
frying pan
TURN BURNER ON **HIGH**, &
brown chops quickly on both sides. THEN:

Lay chops on bottom of a **casserole dish.**
(SAVE SKILLET & OIL. YOU'LL SEE WHY.)

CHOP:
1 med. onion (or use frozen chopped onions)
1 green pepper (always wash fresh vegetables by
rubbing with fingers under running water.

SAUTÉ (fry) them until barely tender. → HAVE BURNER **HOT**,
THEN TURN TO **MEDIUM**

ADD TO THIS:
1 can Campbell's Cream of Mushroom Soup
½ can (5¼ oz.) water
½ teasp. Worcestershire sauce

**STIR WELL &
POUR OVER
CHOPS IN
CASSEROLE.**

**Bake at 350°
Till BUBBLY!**

Serve with :
Green Giant frozen
broccoli spears
(they come seasoned, in a
cooking pouch), sliced
tomatoes, and applesauce.

⑪

Ribs mit sauerkraut

FOR TWO

You need a huge skillet (frying pan) with a lid for this one:

Buy enough **spareribs** (pork) for two (about 2 lbs.)

Leave them in big hunk(s). (They're easy to cut up after they're cooked.)

Salt and pepper them heavily.

Lay them in the bottom of the skillet.

Cover them with **sauerkraut** (a 16 oz. can is enough for two people.)

Add **water** almost to the top of the sauerkraut. **Put lid on.**

Turn burner underneath to **high**, until the whole deal bubbles. Then turn to **simmer**.

Keep covered! **Cook for 2 hours.**

SERVE WITH INSTANT MASHED POTATOES, (BUTTERED); APPLESAUCE; AND HARD ROLLS.

Too colorless? Add a red spiced apple to each plate, at the edge of the applesauce. (OR ADD SOMETHING GREEN, LIKE PARSLEY)

Don't say you don't like sauerkraut until you've tried this!

HaM

Economical:

Buy a **picnic ham**, and even though it says on the label: "Fully cooked and ready to eat," NEVERTHELESS, if you will:

 Cover with boiling water (put lid on pan) and BOIL FOR ONE HOUR,

You'll have the tenderest, juiciest ham you ever tasted! ✳

CUT OFF THE FAT WHEN SLICING OR HUNKING IT. ↓

Ham can be served hot or cold, by itself or combined with other ingredients (see below.)

← SUN. NiGHT iDea ↓ ↓ ↓

Little hunks of cooked ham are delicious in scrambled eggs.

Serve with Quick Grits & applesauce.

✳The only trouble with this method is that lots of vitamins will be left in the water! - so SAVE IT. Pour it into clean cans, cover with foil, and store in refrig. or freezer. (Fat will rise to top of can, and can be scraped off before using.) This water is excellent to dilute ham and green pea soup, which can be bought frozen or canned.

HAM IS GREAT WITH STEAMED CABBAGE (see recipe) ROLLS, AND SLICED TOMATOES

HaM CasseRole : Preheat oven to 350°

Lay in the bottom of a casserole:

 SLICES OR HUNKS OF PICNIC HAM (doesn't have to be boiled first)

On top of that, spread a scanty layer of:

 THIN SLICES OF RAW ONION RINGS (SEPARATED)

On top of that, spread a layer of:

 SLICES OF RAW POTATOES (SLICE THIN)

On top of that, spread undiluted

 ½ CAN CREAM OF MUSHROOM SOUP

Serve with slices of pineapple and tossed salad (p. 29)

REPEAT LAYERS. COVER CASSEROLE DISH

BAKE AT 350° FOR 45 MINUTES.

(Extra yummy: Sprinkle grated cheese on top or between layers.)

⑬

FOR 2,
HALF THIS RECIPE

Pre-heat oven to 350°

RUB VEG. OIL ON BOTTOM OF 9X13 PAN
Rinse under running water:

THE CUT-UP PIECES OF ONE FRYER

Sprinkle the pieces generously with:

POULTRY SEASONING & GROUND BLACK PEPPER

Put chicken in pan, skin side down.
SPREAD WITH
SPOON: **UNDILUTED CREAM OF CHICKEN SOUP**
over the top of the chicken pieces.
(Use one can of soup for one chicken.)

BAKE UNCOVERED (350°) FOR ONE HOUR

Good with canned
green beans, instant
potatoes, and tossed
salad with blue
cheese dressing
(p. 28)

Turn the chicken
over, once, when
half done.

Just before serving:

SPRINKLE WITH SALT

Makes its own
gravy and browns
itself!

HALF-
SMOTHERED
CHICKEN

14

OVEN-FRIED CHICKEN

enough for
2 meals (for 2)

Rinse and dry between paper towels:

2½ LB. BROILER-FRYER CHICKEN

(Buy it already cut up in pieces)

Sprinkle with:

1 TEASPOON SALT

Use:

¼ CUP CHIFFON MARGARINE

to rub entire surface of each piece with.
(Then wipe your _fingers_ on paper towels!)

Roll chicken pieces in:

⅔ CUP CORN FLAKES, CRUSHED INTO CRUMBS

(or any seasoned bread crumbs)

Place pieces, skin-side-up, in baking pan
(15½ x 10½ x 1 inch) lined with foil.

BAKE AT 425° (preheated) 45 MINUTES

(or until tender when stuck with a fork)

Do not turn!

> Good with Green Giant frozen
> Broccoli in cheese Sauce
> (just drop the pouch in boiling water)
> fresh squash, and rolls

⑮

LADYBUG CHICKEN for two

(Nobody knows how it got its name)

MORE CHICKEN RECIPES ON P. 48

INTO THE BOTTOM OF A CASSEROLE, PUT:

½ cup Comet raw rice

ON TOP OF THAT, DISTRIBUTE:

Chicken pieces for two people
Buy all breasts — or whatever your favorite pieces are.

OVER THAT, DROP BLOBS OF

½ tub of Chiffon margarine
(or one stick of other margarine)

THEN POUR IN:

1 cup of water (You may add more later, if needed.)

SPRINKLE OVER TOP:

½ pkg. Lipton's Onion Soup Mix

(Pour the whole package out into a measuring cup, stir it around with a fork so the seasonings will be evenly distributed, then take out approximately half. Save the other half for another day.)

Bake at 350° — 1 hour
(preheated)

Check once, halfway through or later, to see if you need to add water.

SERVE WITH (FROZEN) MIXED VEGETABLES

16

SaLMON CRoQueTTes

Before you start, have about
1 cup of seasoned mashed potatoes
ready. (You can use instant.)

DRaiN:

1 small can salmon
AND FLAKE IT OUT WITH A FORK
INTO A MIXING BOWL.

ADD: an equal amount of mashed potatoes (seasoned)

Take: one egg
AND SEPARATE THE WHITE FROM THE YOLK (YELLOW)

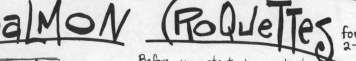

(Catch the yolk in half of the
egg shell. Let the white drool out
into a clean mixing bowl.)
(Save the yolks!)

BEAT THE WHITE TILL
IT IS STIFF. Then add
yolk and beat again
(with the white) until
stiff.

Then gently stir the
salmon and potato
mixture in with egg.

IF IT SEEMS TOO RUNNY
TO HOLD TOGETHER, ADD
3 soda crackers, crumbled fine.
(or more if necessary.)

THEN:

TURN BURNER ON HIGH. COVER BOTTOM OF A
SKILLET WITH THIN LAYER OF MAZOLA OR WESSON OIL.

Drop a big spoonful of salmon mixture into
hot skillet. (Flatten slightly with spatula.) Each
spoonful makes a lighter-than-air croquette.

COOK FOUR AT A TIME. BROWN ON EACH SIDE.

Serve with lemon slices.

Good with green beans and tossed salad.

TUNa FoR TWo

This recipe is best
made with noodles,
but if you don't have
time to make a couple
of cups of cooked noodles,
then, as a substitute:

OPeN:

1 can. (15 oz.) Franco-
American MACARONI
with cheese sauce

**AND SPREAD HALF OF IT INTO BOTTOM
OF A CASSEROLE.** You will need a casserole
that holds more than one quart.

THEN OPEN: 1 SMALL CAN OF TUNa

DIG HALF OF IT OUT WITH A FORK AND ARRANGE
IT ON TOP OF MACARONI (OR NOODLES)

*Then put rest of can of macaroni
on top of that.*

THEN PUT REST OF TUNA ON TOP OF THAT!

Now, on top of those layers, **SPReaD:** (with a spoon)

3/4 CAN OF (UNDILUTED) MUSHROOM SOUP

NO NEED TO STIR

TOP WITH CRUMBLED-UP POTATO CHIPs - OR
CORN FLAKES OR CRACKER CRUMBS

Bake aT 400-450° UNTIL TOP is BROWN
20 MIN OR MORE

Serve with mixed vegetables (buy frozen) and rolls.

VARY RECIPE WITH SMALL AMT. OF CURRY POWDER (mixed into soup.)

FOOLPROOF FISH

for two

If your husband is a fisherman, you're lucky! — Because the only secret to cooking delectable fish is to have FRESH fish. (Besides that, he who catches, <u>cleans</u>.) This recipe is foolproof for almost any kind of fresh fish: small bass, perch, etc.

PREHEAT OVEN - 350°

Lay cleaned fish in greased oven pan (preferably one that will double as a serving dish).

SCORE THE FISH
— which means: make shallow slashes with a sharp knife across the top of the fish, like this:

SQUEEZE LEMON JUICE OVER THE FISH
(¼-½ lemon per fish — depends on you)

DOT THE FISH WITH LITTLE GLOBS OF BUTTER

Bake 20 - 30 Min

WHEN YOU <u>SMELL</u> FISH, iT'S DONE! SERVE WITH LEMON WEDGES.

broiled zucchini (p.22)
Good with tossed salad, ∧ and corn sticks or hush puppies, which you can buy frozen.

Fix-ahead **FONDUE** for **TWO**

(with enough left over for lunch the next day)

You need a 9×13 (2" deep) all-purpose baking dish.
RUB SOME MARGARINE ON THE SIDES AND BOTTOM OF IT, THEN:

Pull or cut crusts off of:
7 slices of bread

Spread:
Soft margarine on one side of bread.
Put "buttered" side down (in pan)
(CUTTING UP LAST PIECE AS NEEDED TO MAKE A GOOD FIT).

Lay:
7 slices of sharp cheese
on top of bread slices (OR,
INSTEAD, YOU CAN SPRINKLE ABOUT 6 OZ.
[1½ CUPS] OF READY-GRATED CHEESE
ON TOP) Be sure cheese is marked
"NATURAL" on the package.

On top of that, sprinkle:
3 Tablespoons of chopped onions
(FRESH GREEN, OR FROZEN CHOPPED)

IN A BIG BOWL,
Beat:
3 eggs (all together) till frothy

Add to eggs: **3 cups of milk** (homogenized)
3/4 teaspoon dry mustard (mild)
3/4 teaspoon salt and stir together.

Pour this mixture over bread, cheese, and onions
in pan, and:
COVER WITH PLASTIC WRAP OR WAX PAPER AND
Let stand for 2 hours or longer in refrig.

BAKE FOR 45-50 MIN. AT 350°

Serve with tossed green salad (p.29) **and**
fruity dessert (p.32)

20

CHEESE PIE

GRATE (or buy already grated):

½ lb. (2 cups) Swiss cheese

ON A BIG PIECE OF WAX PAPER, SPRINKLE:

1 Tablespoon flour

Roll the cheese around in the flour until it has taken it all up.

SPRINKLE CHEESE INTO:

9" unbaked pastry shell (buy it frozen).

BEAT WELL IN MIXING BOWL:
3 eggs

MIX IN WITH THE EGGS:

1 cup milk
¼ teaspoon salt
4 grinds of black pepper

POUR MIXTURE OVER CHEESE.

Bake in oven preheated at

400° for 15 min.
Then reduce heat to

300° for 30 min.

Stick a knife in center of pie. If blade comes out _clean_, pie is done!

GREAT with FROZEN ASPARAGUS and TOSSED SALAD (p. 29)

21

Zippy Zucchini

Serves 4 — or
serves 2, twice

Into a casserole put:

½ cup MINUTE RICE (uncooked)

Stir into rice:

1 can (16 oz.) ZUCCHINI SQUASH (use liquid)

Sprinkle on top:

¼-½ cup GRATED CHEESE (Kraft's natural cheddar, ready-grated)
(about 1 oz.)

COVER THE CASSEROLE.

COOK aT 350° FOR 20 MIN.
- or until cheese has melted.

BROILED ZUCCHINI:
BOILED &
FOR TWO

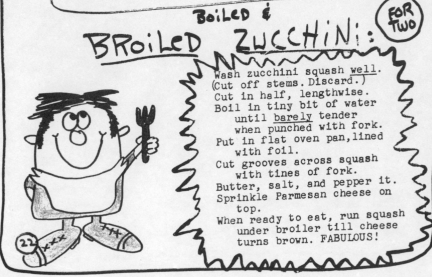

Wash zucchini squash well.
(Cut off stems. Discard.)
Cut in half, lengthwise.
Boil in tiny bit of water
    until <u>barely</u> tender
    when punched with fork.
Put in flat oven pan, lined
    with foil.
Cut grooves across squash
    with tines of fork.
Butter, salt, and pepper it.
Sprinkle Parmesan cheese on
    top.
When ready to eat, run squash
    under broiler till cheese
    turns brown. FABULOUS!

22

FRESH!

FRESH SQUASH
for two

SELECT SEVERAL SMALL, FIRM SQUASH.

(Avoid the ones with dry, black stems)

RINSE THOROUGHLY UNDER RUNNING WATER, RUBBING SQUASH WITH YOUR FINGERS TO REMOVE ALL TRACE OF SAND.

Good Source of VITAMIN A

CUT OFF STEMS AND DISCARD.

CUT SQUASH INTO PIECES – ANY SIZE OR SHAPE.

DROP INTO PAN OF BOILING, SALTED WATER.

(Not much water – about 1/8 cup, or just enough to keep squash from sticking to pan while cooking.)

(Not too much salt: 1/4 -1/2 teaspoon, depending on how much squash. "You can always add more salt!"

Turn burner from HIGH to LOW after water resumes boiling.

COVER PAN. BOIL ON LOW OR SIMMER TILL SQUASH IS TENDER WHEN PUNCHED WITH FORK.

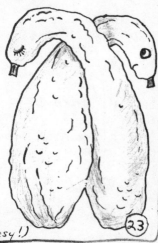

When ready to serve, dump squash in strainer and add a glob of butter or margarine before serving.

VARIATION: Add 1/2 can Cheddar Cheese Soup after draining. Return to pan to heat through. CAN ALSO ADD ONION AND/OR TOBASCO SAUCE. (But go easy!)

23

Sweet & Sour

A vegetable
or salad.
SERVE COLD.

Beans

– for a party!

Goes great
with picnic
supper!
(See below)

*Make this at least
a day ahead. It keeps
a week or longer in the refrigerator, and gets
better all the time. This recipe will make you famous!*

MIX TOGETHER:
(in a large mixing bowl)

½ cup oil (Mazola, Wesson, etc.)
½ cup vinegar
½ cup (or less) sugar

OPEN & DRAIN:

1 can (16 oz) cut wax beans
1 can (16 oz.) French-cut green beans
1 can (16 oz.) kidney beans. Use the
best brand available and rinse
under cold, running water. (Use a strainer or colander.)
ADD THE BEANS TO THE MIXING BOWL

CHOP UP: (VERY FINE)

(about half a cup)
1 small green pepper (Rinse first by holding under cold, running
water and rubbing with thumbs. Then remove stem and insides.
1 small onion – any kind, making about ⅓ cup   (DISCARD)
(But first remove outer skin by cutting off stem end and peeling)

ADD TO MIXING BOWL. COVER & REFRIGERATE. (Stir First)

GOOD WITH SLICES OF HAM, CHEESE, & RYE BREAD

COOKING TIME:
35-40 MIN.

Vanishing Vegetables

PUT 'EM ON THE TABLE
AND WATCH 'EM DISAPPEAR!

Melt over **LOW** heat in a big stew pot:

¼ lb. margarine

Chop up (but not too small):

1 large onion
1 large green pepper

ADD THEM TO MELTED MARGARINE & COOK ON **MED.**
UNTIL THEY ARE BARELY LIMP (a couple of minutes?)
Then add:

2 pkgs. (10 oz. each) **frozen corn** (whole Kernel)

TURN HEAT TO **LOW** AND COVER PAN
Cook 15 min., stirring as needed
Cut into fourths and add to pan:

5 fresh tomatoes (med. or large) (slightly green)

Also add:

1 pkg. (10 oz.) frozen cut okra
2 teaspoons salt
fresh ground pepper - 20 or so cranks

Simmer 20 more minutes.
TRANSFER TO LARGE CASSEROLE AND KEEP
IN WARM OVEN TILL EATING TIME

Great with ham!

25

Broccoli 'N' Onion Casserole

 SERVES FOUR

 CUT IN HALF FOR 2

Drop in boiling water:

2 pkgs. frozen BROCCOLI SPEARS in cooking pouches

When done according to directions on package,
Empty contents of pouches into large casserole.

Drain:

1 can (8oz.) TINY ONIONS

and bury them among the broccoli spears

Then combine:

3/4 cup MAYONNAISE (Hellman's or Kraft's)

with:

1 Tablespoon HORSERADISH (you'll find this with refrigerated foods at the market.)

and spread mixture over top of broccoli and onions

Sprinkle on top:

1/2 cup grated CHEDDAR CHEESE (You can buy Kraft's, already grated, in plastic bags.)

Bake at **350°** until cheese is melted.

You should serve at least one cooked, green leafy vegetable every day. (If your husband doesn't get one with lunch, be sure he gets one with the evening meal.)

The frozen greens are good: spinach, turnip greens, mustard greens, etc., and buying them frozen saves much time and work.

However, one of the best green, leafy vegetables

- AND SO ECONOMICAL! -

is _fresh_ cabbage (not frozen) which is quick and easy to cook.

HINT: Keep cabbage wrapped and in the refrigerator before cooking, to preserve vitamins.

WHAT? YOU NEVER LIKED CABBAGE? THEN IT WAS COOKED WRONG! (A strong flavor develops in cabbage ONLY when it is improperly cooked and its sulfur compounds are broken down, causing unpleasant cooking odors and (later) gas on the tummy.

SO HEED THESE DIRECTIONS!

FOR TWO

STeaMeD CaBBaGe

Remove the outer leaves from a well-chilled (SMALL SIZE)
HeaD OF CaBBaGe
and cut it in half. Now shred it fine, as for cole slaw. If you don't have a shredder, use a knife and chopping board. (CUT CABBAGE INTO FOURTHS, THEN SLICE VERY THIN.)
PuT CaBBaGe iNTo SauCepaN
ADD 2 TABLESPOONS OF BoiLiNG WaTeR and
place on HIGH heat and cover. When lid is hot, turn to simmer. (Takes less than a minute, usually.)
SiMMeR FOR 8 MiNuTes
Then stir in margarine (lots!) and salt and fresh-ground pepper
SeRVe iMMeDiaTeLY

SALAD TIPS:

(1) Buy really GREEN lettuce that looks fresh. The greener the leaves, the more nutritious the salad! Get several kinds if possible and use a little of each for party salads.

(2) Keep lettuce in plastic bag in refrigerator. (Keeps better unwashed.)

(3) On day you plan to use it, rinse lettuce thoroughly under cold, running water (washing both sides of each leaf). NEVER SOAK VEGETABLES! (Destroys vitamins.) Drain in colander.

(4) Dry the clean lettuce between paper towels or clean dish towels.

(5) Store in <u>clean</u> plastic bag with paper towel in bottom to absorb extra moisture, and keep refrigerated.

(6) When ready to use, tear lettuce into bite-size pieces.

BLUE CHEESE DRESSING:

With a fork, crumble up (in a small mixing bowl):

3 oz. blue cheese (½ cup, crumbled)

Blend in with spoon:

¼ cup mayonnaise (Kraft or Hellman's)

Gradually add:

½ cup buttermilk

Mix well, adding

Salt to taste

Cover and refrigerate

Ladle over individual bowls of lettuce. No tossing necessary.

Tossed Green Salad

Your clean lettuce must be DRY.
Then, just before serving:

① TOSS FIRST WITH JUST THE SALAD OIL, until every leaf is glistening.

② THEN ADD LEMON JUICE OR VINEGAR and seasonings.

> REASON: Oil seals out air and holds in vitamins AND prevents salt from drawing out moisture from lettuce (which would destroy crispness).

Salad DRESSING FOR Two:

1 Tablespoon of salad oil (Mazola, Wesson, etc.)
¼ lemon (about 1½ teaspoons) - or same amt. of vinegar
⅛ teaspoon salt

> Vary the amounts of oil, lemon (or vinegar), and salt to suit individual taste. Also, you can add fresh-ground black pepper.

Add any or all (or none): - Tomatoes, celery, cucumbers, raw carrots, green peppers, and radishes — chopped up. These are good when fixed the day before and marinated overnight in its own salad dressing and left, covered, in refrigerator. Drain and add vegetables at last minute to the salad (which has first been tossed in its own dressing.)

> A GREAT, FRESH-TASTING SALAD CAN BE MADE WITH JUST LETTUCE, DRESSING, AND A CUP (OR MORE) OF COTTAGE CHEESE, TOSSED IN AT LAST MINUTE.

Like avocados? Wash, peel, and slice. Add last.

> Be sure your bowl is plenty big, to allow tossing without spilling.

TOSS GENTLY →

GRaPeFRuiT CuP SaLaD for two

(always chill fruit (except bananas) as soon as you buy it.)

← Cut a grapefruit in half.

Then, with a grapefruit Knife (or sharp-pointed spoon) scoop out sections of grapefruit, and put them in a mixing bowl.

Remove pulp from inside of grapefruit shells with grapefruit Knife and discard.

OPTIONAL: With sharp Knife, scallop edges of empty grapefruit shells

Into the bowl containing grapefruit sections, mix Canned fruit cocktail or any fresh fruits in season: strawberries, melons (scooped out in round balls) grapes, peaches, cherries, etc. Any combination!

Drain juice off and pile fruit into grapefruit shells. Top with Poppyseed Dressing. Serve on salad plates plain or on a washed leaf of lettuce.

POPPY SEED DRESSING (Makes nearly 2 cups)

PUT THE FOLLOWING IN A SMALLISH BOWL:

- 1 teaspoon salt
- 1 teaspoon dry mustard
- 1 teaspoon paprika
- ½ cup white corn syrup
- ⅓ cup vinegar
- 1 cup corn oil

OPTIONAL: → 1½ Tablespoons onion juice →(HIGHLY RECOMMENDED)

Beat with egg beater (or mixer on MED.) until well blended and thickened. Add:

- 1½ Tablespoons poppy seeds

and beat a few more times. Put in covered jar and keep refrigerated. Serve over any fruit salad.

FRENCH DRESSING that you will be remembered for!

In the bottom of a small bowl, with the back of a spoon,
MASH:
A CLOVE OF GARLIC (peel husk off first!)
and add a pinch of salt to hold it all together.

In a bigger bowl, MIX:

- 1 cup Wesson Oil
- ½ cup vinegar
- ½ Tablespoon lemon juice
- ½ teaspoon salt
- 1 teaspoon curry powder
- 3/4 teaspoon paprika
- ½ teaspoon dry mustard

including garlic clove

Put it all into a bottle, Shake before using. When pouring over salad, be sure not to pour out mashed garlic clove or you will be remembered too well!

This recipe is to be used when you're having company and are too nervous to mix your own salad dressing at the last minute (as recommended on page 29 for most occasions.) Use this prepared mixture just before tossing and serving salad.

31

FRUITY SALAD

WITH SOUR CREAM
(Serves 8)

Doubles as a dessert

a GOOD PARTY- PARTY- DISH

MIX TOGETHER:

8 oz. **sour cream**

can of **pineapple tidbits**
    (13-14 oz. POUR OFF JUICE)

large can **fruit cocktail**

can of **Mandarin orange** segments
    (about 11 oz.)

– and – optional –

as many miniature **marshmallows**
as you like

COVER AND KEEP CHILLED

Good with "oven-fried" chicken and zucchini casserole!

See p. 15 & p. 22

TOMATO ASPIC MOLD for a party (SERVES 8)

First, rub the inside of a clean

8" ring mold with salad oil. Then

Open:

a **46 oz.** (nearly 2 quarts) **can Libby's tomato juice**
and:

Pour 1 cup of the juice out into measuring cup.
Into that, sprinkle contents of:

3 envelopes of Knox (unflavored) gelatine
so gelatine will soften.

In a big saucepan, heat remaining juice
(nearly 5 cups) to boiling point, but don't boil.
Then:

Add softened cup of gelatine to the hot juice. STIR WELL.
Also add:

the juice of half a lemon (or less)
3 teaspoons salt
1 cup (or more) of **"salad olives"** (cut-up stuffed olives)

Pour into mold. Cover with wax paper or foil. Refrigerate.
(It takes at least six hours to set.)

TO GET ASPIC OUT OF MOLD:

After aspic is set,
turn mold upside down
on platter and rub a
clean, hot, wet cloth
over bottom of mold.
Tap mold with knife
handle. If aspic
doesn't drop free,
use a knife (not a
sharp-pointed one)
to work edges
of aspic loose.
If you are not
going to eat it
right away, cover
it and return it
to refrigerator.

Fill center with
**chive
cottage cheese**

Surround aspic
with washed
leaves of
lettuce

(33)

BAKED POTATOES
There's nothing easier.

400° - 1 hour

Wash them first, of course, and cut out any bad spots. Then put them right on the rack in your preheated oven (you don't even need a pan!) and leave them there for an hour. When you take them out, prick them with a fork to let steam escape.

Serve with margarine and/or sour cream, and of course salt and pepper.

BAKED BEANS
Mix together: (In baking dish)

1 can (16 oz.) Campbell's Pork & Beans
3½ oz. Catsup
2 oz. brown sugar
1/4 onion, chopped fine
strip of bacon, cut-up, on top.

BAKE 4 HOURS AT 325°

FRENCH OR SOUR-DOUGH BREAD
for a party

Buy a loaf of French Bread (or Sour Dough Bread) (already baked) and slice it thickly - but don't slice it quite all the way through to the bottom.

Spread soft margarine (like chiffon) on one side of each slice and then close loaf back up (by pushing all the slices close together). Want garlic bread? Add garlic salt to margarine.

Wrap with foil, and when ready to heat, open foil a little bit at the top of loaf and put it in oven till bread is hot and crunchy.

You can use almost any temperature setting between 300°-450.° If you're not using your oven for anything else:
400° - 15-20 min.

(34)

Want individual slices? Put 'em unbuttered in toaster.

No-BeaT PoPoVeRs

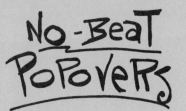

Every hostess needs to be able to cook one special thing that sets her apart. Want something so easy you won't believe it? Try this:

> THE **SECRET:**
> START WITH A COLD OVEN

Mix well (in a bowl with a spoon) — (DISREGARDING LUMPS):

> 2 EGGS
> 1 CUP MILK
> 1 CUP (after sifting) FLOUR
> ½ teasp. SALT

Grease a muffin tin **well**.

Fill 8 cups ¾ full

PUT IN 450° OVEN (not preheated)

BAKE 30 MINUTES & DON'T PEEK!

Serve immediately. (You are now famous.)

PuMPKiN
iCe-CReaM
Pie

HeLP!

1 quart vanilla ice milk

Leave out until it's soft.   Then:

PUT IT IN LARGE MIXING BOWL WITH:

1 can. (16 oz.) **pumpkin** (Libby's Solid Pack)
½ cup brown sugar
⅛ teaspoon   salt
2 teaspoons pumpkin pie spice

MIX WELL AND POUR INTO:

9" **graham cracker pie shell**, (which you
can buy ready-to-use at supermarket)

Cover with Saran Wrap and
         FREEZE TILL FIRM or longer.

Serve frozen. Leftover pie can be kept
indefinitely in freezer.

Speedy Icebox Pie

MIX: (with a fork, in a bowl)

8 oz. PKG. PHILADELPHIA CREAM CHEESE

with:

i CAN (13-15 oz.) CRUSHED PINEAPPLE, drained

MIX INTO THAT: ½ CARTON OF COOL WHIP
(pint-size, Birdseye, in frozen food section)

STIR IN: ½ of a 7-oz. can or package of SHREDDED COCONUT

SMUSH this mixture into a graham cracker "READY-CRUST" pie shell

(WHICH YOU BUY, ALREADY PREPARED, IN A FOIL PAN AT YOUR SUPERMARKET.)

SPREAD OTHER ½ OF COOL WHIP ON TOP

SEPARATELY: put other half of shredded coconut on a piece of foil in oven and brown quickly under broiler. Sprinkle this coconut over top of already-prepared pie. Cover with Saran Wrap and REFRIGERATE. TASTES BETTER IF WHOLE PIE HAS A FEW HOURS TO "SET" IN REFRIGERATOR.

Counting calories? Substitute Krafts CALORIE-WISE CHEESE. Same size + flavor.

CODDLED EGGS

Better than soft-boiled!

NO COOKING OR TIMING REQUIRED

All you need is boiling water!

PUT 4 EGGS (in their shells) **IN A 1-QT. SAUCEPAN**

FILL PAN WITH BOILING WATER
(Pan shouldn't be on burner)

COVER PAN WITH TIGHT-FITTING LID

LEAVE ANY LENGTH OF TIME (over 10 min.)

If you have left the eggs for so long you are afraid they will be cold, do this: A minute or two before you are ready to eat, fill bowls you plan to eat from with boiling water, and let eggs (still in shells) stand in this a minute. Just before serving, pour off water, and eggs and bowl will be hot.

SERVE WITH WHOLE WHEAT TOAST, WHICH MAY BE CRUMBLED UP IN BOWL WITH EGGS (IF NO ONE OBJECTS.)

Want to fix only two eggs? Same directions -- just don't cover saucepan.

SUGGESTION
Since eggs tarnish silver, use stainless steel utensils to eat them with, if possible. In any case, always remove leftover egg from dishes and silverware immediately (before washing dishes), using cold water and a vegetable brush, like the one the Fuller Brush man gives-away; they're the best!

38

SCRAMBLED EGGS

Crack open as many eggs as you want to eat into a mixing bowl and beat lightly with a fork. Put small amount of vegetable oil (a teaspoon or more) in frying pan (I hope it's Teflon) and heat pan. Pour eggs into pan and turn heat to LOW. NEVER SALT EGGS UNTIL YOU'RE READY TO EAT THEM. When eggs begin to thicken, break them up as they cook with a wooden or plastic spoon (or fork-spoon) and keep stirring until they are done to the consistency you like. Serve immediately.

When you want to get fancy, add bits of chopped ham or cooked sausage or crumbled cheese to eggs while they're cooking.

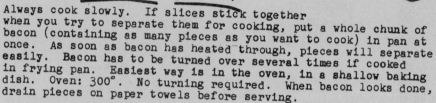

COOKING BACON

Always cook slowly. If slices stick together when you try to separate them for cooking, put a whole chunk of bacon (containing as many pieces as you want to cook) in pan at once. As soon as bacon has heated through, pieces will separate easily. Bacon has to be turned over several times if cooked in frying pan. Easiest way is in the oven, in a shallow baking dish. Oven: 300°. No turning required. When bacon looks done, drain pieces on paper towels before serving.

FRENCH TOAST (FOR TWO)

In a big bowl, with a fork, BEAT LIGHTLY:

2 eggs

STIR IN: **¼ cup milk**

ADD: **Pinch of salt** (½ teaspoon)

Grease griddle (or frying pan) lightly with salad oil, wiping off excess with paper towels.
Have griddle hot, on 450° or MEDIUM HIGH

Dip one slice of bread at a time (as you are ready to cook them) into egg mixture so that both sides have a coating. (DON'T SOAK.)

Put coated bread on hot griddle, turning only once, WHEN IT IS DONE ON THE BOTTOM SIDE (lift up edge of bread and peek.)

Serve with butter and syrup - or cinnamon sugar.

PANCAKES & WAFFLES
Buy frozen or buy the mix.

COFFEE
Buy freeze-dried instant.

HERE'S WHAT YOU NEED TO BUY

↓

IF YOU ARE GOING TO FIX THAT

From Frozen Foods Section:

1 package Pepperidge Farm Patty Shells

4 packages "Chicken Sara Lee" ✱

2 packages Stouffer's <u>au gratin potatoes</u>

Frozen (cooked) Brownies <u>or</u> cake

(<u>NOT FROZEN</u>): - Head of lettuce

Chiffon margarine + jelly or jam

1 package BROWN-&-SERVE ROLLS
(preferably in alum. foil pan)

1 can (1 lb. 4 oz.) fruit cocktail

1 small bottle of Ginger Ale

instant coffee or tea, lemon or milk + sugar

✱ OR - (less expensive) 2 (10½ oz.) cans or one large can SWANSON'S CHICKEN A LA KING

Fix-aHead
DiNNeR PaRTY FoR 4

☞ ## MeNU:

Chicken Sara Lee in patty shells
(↑HAS WATER CHESTNUTS, MUSHROOMS, + PEAS)

Potatoes au gratin (COOK AS DIRECTED ON PACKAGE)

Easy frozen fruit salad (DIRECTIONS BELOW)

Rolls & jam

Iced tea or hot coffee

Brownies (or cake) ALL YOU HAVE TO DO IS THAW THIS

DRAIN can of **FRUIT COCKTAIL**
and dump fruit into
empty ice tray. (Remove
dividers first.)

POUR ON TOP of fruit:
1 small bottle of
ginger ale.

Put tray in freezing
compartment for several
hours or longer (until
ready to serve.) You
will be cutting this
frozen fruit salad into
big squares and arranging
them on lettuce leaves when
ready to serve.

BAKE AHEAD: Frozen patty shells, as directed
on box.

HEAT CHICKEN SARA LEE as directed on box
and fill patty shells at last minute.

Party Girl

EASTER
DINNER

directions ☞

FOR TWO

MENU:

Ham with apricot **sauce** surrounded on the platter by:

☆ **Pineapple rings** with crabapple centers!

☆ **Sweet potatoes**

☆ **Green beans** with toasted almonds

☆ **Hot rolls** (store-bought)

DESSERT:
(made the day before)

Speedy icebox pie *
-or-
☆ **Easter cake**
(bought at the bakery)

*See recipe

42

DiRECTiONS
FOR THaT MeNU

Happy Easter egg!

Heat a small canned ham according to directions on can. While it is cooking, mix together in a small bowl:

> ½ cup apricot jam
> ¼ teaspoon salt
> 1 Tablespoon water

(You will put this sauce over ham during its last 20 minutes of cooking.)

COOK BIRDSEYE FROZ. FRENCH-CUT GREEN BEANS WITH TOASTED ALMONDS as directed on package.

Open a small
Can of pineapple slices (rings). DRAIN. Then open a small
Can of whole sweet potatoes. DRAIN, and cut them in half (lengthwise).
Also open a small
Jar of canned, spiced crab apples. DRAIN.

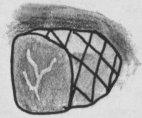

20 min. before ham is done, take it out of oven and cut slashes on outside as shown.

SPREaD aPRiCOT MiXTURe OVER TOP OF HaM aND SURROUND HaM WiTH **SWeeT POTaTOeS** aND **PiNeaPbLe SLices** WiTH **CRaB aPPLes IN CeNTeRS** (of pineapples).

Put the ham, etc. back in the oven for last 20 min.

Serve ham on hot platter, surrounded by fruit + potatoes

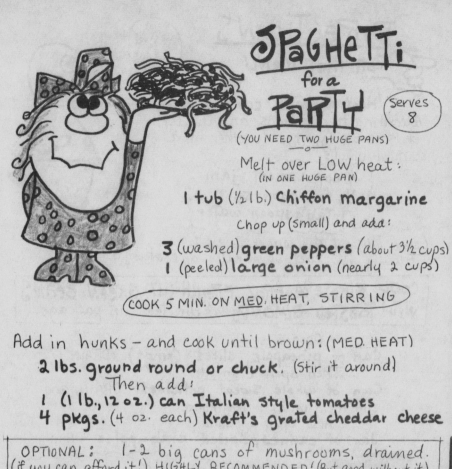

SPAGHETTI
for a
PARTY

Serves 8

(YOU NEED TWO HUGE PANS)

Melt over LOW heat:
(IN ONE HUGE PAN)

1 tub (½ lb.) Chiffon margarine

Chop up (small) and add:

3 (washed) green peppers (about 3½ cups)
1 (peeled) large onion (nearly 2 cups)

COOK 5 MIN. ON MED. HEAT, STIRRING

Add in hunks — and cook until brown: (MED. HEAT)

2 lbs. ground round or chuck. (Stir it around)
Then add:
1 (1 lb., 12 oz.) can Italian style tomatoes
4 pkgs. (4 oz. each) **Kraft's grated cheddar cheese**

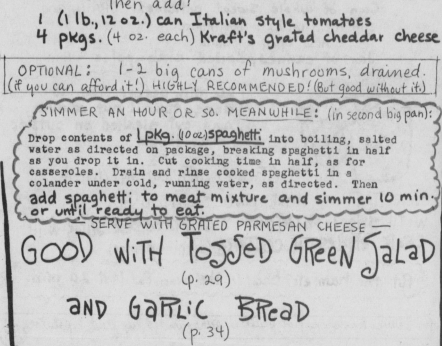

OPTIONAL: 1-2 big cans of mushrooms, drained.
(if you can afford it!) HIGHLY RECOMMENDED! (But good without it!)

SIMMER AN HOUR OR SO. MEANWHILE: (in second big pan):

Drop contents of **1 pkg. (10 oz.) spaghetti** into boiling, salted water as directed on package, breaking spaghetti in half as you drop it in. Cut cooking time in half, as for casseroles. Drain and rinse cooked spaghetti in a colander under cold, running water, as directed. Then **add spaghetti to meat mixture and simmer 10 min. or until ready to eat.**

— SERVE WITH GRATED PARMESAN CHEESE —

GOOD WITH TOSSED GREEN SALAD
(p. 29)

and GARLIC BREAD
(p. 34)

THANKSGIVING OR CHRISTMAS
Feast for two

MENU:

Turkey - cooked the quick way
Dressing - fixed ahead of time
Gravy - easy!
Cranberry Sauce - open a can.
Green bean & pea casserole - fixed ahead
Sweet potatoes - fixed ahead
Grapefruit salad - fixed ahead
Rolls - store-bought
Pumpkin ice cream pie - fixed ahead

DIRECTIONS ON NEXT TWO PAGES →

TURKEY & dressing

(1) Buy a 12 to 14 pound turkey hen in plenty of time for Christmas to allow for thorough thawing, if it's frozen. (This may take 2-3 days in refrigerator.)

(2) Remove neck and giblets from body cavity, after turkey is defrosted. If inside is still slightly frozen, run some water inside. If you don't want to fool with giblets, give them to the neighbor's cat. If you have time, however, boil them for an hour or so in salty water and chop them up to add to gravy.

(3) Rinse turkey quickly inside and out under running water and pat dry with paper towels.

(4) Spread out a long sheet of 18" heavy duty Reynolds Wrap aluminum foil and rub it with soft margarine.

(5) Place turkey in middle of foil, breast side up.

(6) Smear soft margarine all over topside of turkey.

(7) Tear off some extra patches of foil, double them, and put them over ends of legs and wing tips so they won't puncture outside wrapping.

(8) Fold foil around turkey - loosely (not airtight).

(9) Put in shallow flat pan in oven preheated to 450°.

(10) After 2 3/4 hours <u>or less</u>, fold back foil and stick a meat thermometer into thickest part of turkey's thigh.

(11) Is it done? (185°) If it's almost done, turn broiler to "BROIL" and let turkey brown just a few minutes, but don't overdo or it will dry meat out.

(12) Didn't brown enough or evenly enough? Rub a little A-1 sauce over the top of the turkey and HE won't know the difference.

FIX-AHEAD DRESSING:

Buy Pepperidge Farm Stuffing Mix, follow the simple directions, and cook in a separate pan. DO NOT STUFF TURKEY. Keep dressing refrigerated till time to reheat.

Fixings for the Feast

Sweet Potato Casserole
(MAKE A DAY OR TWO AHEAD)

MUSH TOGETHER IN MIXING BOWL WITH FORK

- 1 can (16 oz.) mashed sweet potatoes
- 1/4 of a tub of Chiffon, or other soft margarine
- 1/4 teaspoon salt
- 1/2 cup light brown sugar

When it is all blended together, put it in a casserole and sprinkle over the top:

1/4 cup chopped pecans

Cover casserole and refrigerate until ready to heat and eat. (300° for 25-35 minutes.)

How To Make The Gravy
to go with the turkey

Buy a package of McCormick Chicken Gravy Mix and follow the simple directions on the package. Add chopped up giblets (if you have any) and some of the turkey juices collected in the bottom of the pan you cooked the turkey in. That's all! →

Alternate method: ←

Heat an undiluted can of Campbell's Cream of Chicken Soup and add enough turkey drippings to make it the consistency you want. (Save the rest of the drippings to use with leftover turkey.) Want to make gravy from scratch? SEE PAGE 9. But don't use beer.

Fix-ahead Green Bean & Pea Casserole

In a large casserole put:

- 1 tiny can French style green beans or any green beans (drained)
- 1 tiny can of tiny(!) early green peas (drained)

Mix in a bowl:

- ½ can mushroom soup (undiluted)
- 1½ Tablespoons milk → Put over top of vegetables

Crumble on top:

½ can French-fried onion rings (or 1 tiny can if available)

Sprinkle on top of that:

Grated Parmesan Cheese (as much or as little as you like)

Cover casserole and refrigerate until ready to heat and eat. Bake at 300 for 25 minutes AT THE SAME TIME YOU HEAT SWEET POTATO CASSEROLE AND TURKEY DRESSING.

GRAPEFRUIT Salad - see page 30

PUMPKIN ice CREAM PiE - see page 36

WHAT TO DO WITH
LEFTOVER TURKEY
(or chicken) FOR 2
- - - - - - - - - - - - - - - - - - - -

COMBINE, in a casserole:

Leftover turkey or chicken hunks
with:

a small can of tiny Eng. peas
and
a can of Compliment Cooking Sauce.

COVER & BAKE AT 350   - 40 MINUTES
Good with tossed salad.

MIX IN A CASSEROLE:

1 cup leftover turkey hunks (bite-size
1 can celery soup (undiluted)
1 teaspoon curry powder
1/4 green pepper, sliced thin
(no seasoning)

Cover and bake at 350° - 40 min.
This is very good served over Uncle Ben's wild and reg. rice mixture
Serve with broiled zucchini squash (p. 22)

MIX TOGETHER IN CASSEROLE:
Bite-size chunks of leftover turkey
1 (3 oz.) can of mushrooms, drained
½ can cream of mushroom soup, undiluted
2 oz. dry sherry
½ cup sour cream

Cover. Bake at 350° - 40 min. Good served
with Fruity Salad (p. 32)

Partially cook (only) according to directions on package:
1 pkg. (10 oz.) frozen {broccoli spears   } and drain
{or asparagus spears}
Then:
Lay broccoli in bottom of shallow casserole or ovenproof oval
steak platter, and MIX TOGETHER:

½ cup milk
1 can Campbell's celery soup (undiluted)
Pour half of mixture over broccoli, and on top of that, lay:
slices of leftover turkey
and pour rest of soup mixture over turkey slices. Then sprinkle:
½ cup shredded cheddar cheese
on top of everything and bake at 350° for 40 min. Serve with
baked potatoes (p. 34)

Put dry Pepperidge Farm Stuffing Mix
in bottom of a casserole, and
½ can cream of chicken soup on top of that
Then, leftover turkey slices go on top of that, and
the other ½ can of chicken soup goes over all of it. Good
served with green, leafy vegetable.
(Buy frozen.)

350° -
40 MIN.